★ IT'S MY STATE! ★
Kentucky

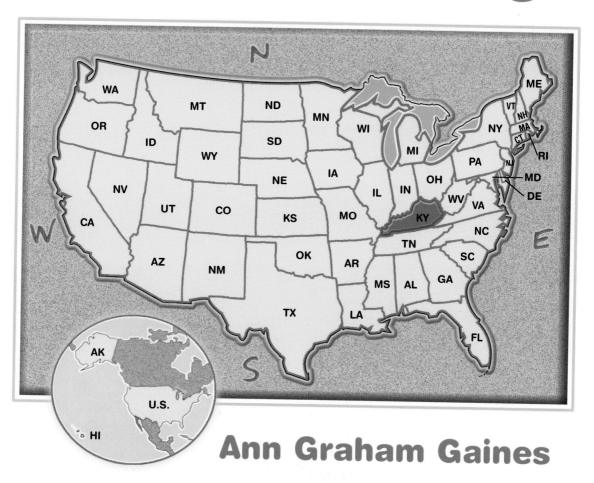

Ann Graham Gaines

BENCHMARK BOOKS

MARSHALL CAVENDISH
NEW YORK

Series Consultant

David G. Vanderstel, Ph.D., Executive Director, National Council on Public History

With thanks to Dr. William Ellis for his expert review of the manuscript.

Benchmark Books
Marshall Cavendish
99 White Plains Road
Tarrytown, New York 10591-9001
www.marshallcavendish.com

Library of Congress Cataloging-in-Publication Data

Gaines, Ann.
Kentucky / by Ann Graham Gaines.
p. cm. — (It's my state!)
Summary: Surveys the history, geography, government, economy, and people
of Kentucky.
Includes bibliographical references (p.) and index.
ISBN 0-7614-1525-4
1. Kentucky—Juvenile literature. [1. Kentucky.]
I. Title. II. Series.

F451.3 .G35 2003
976.9—dc21
2002015072

03/06

Photo research by Candlepants, Inc.

Cover photograph: Annie Griffiths Belt/Corbis

Back cover illustration: The license plate shows Kentucky's postal abbreviation, followed by its year of statehood.

The photographs in this book are used by permission and through the courtesy of: *Corbis:* 5 (middle), 31, 32, 33, 34, 36, 39 (top), 43, 73 (middle); Bettmann, 25, 30, 37, 47 (bottom); Gary W. Carter, 4 (top), 16 (middle); Patrick Johns, 4 (middle); Hal Horwitz, 4 (bottom); Kevin R. Morris, 5 (top), 9, 15, 48, 53, 54, 55, 56, 71, 72 (middle), 72 (bottom), 75; Lester V. Bergman, 5 (bottom); Annie Griffiths Belt, 8, 51; David Muench, 10, 13, 14; W. Cody, 12; Ric Ergenbright, 16 (top), 66; D. Robert & Lorri Franz, 16 (bottom), 17 (bottom); Terry W. Eggers, 17 (top); Roy Morsch, 17 (middle); Kennan Ward, 19; Raymond Gehman, 21, 27, 49, 52, 60, 61, 64; Underwood & Underwood, 34; Stapleton Collection, 39 (bottom), 47 (middle); Mark Peterson, 40; Buddy Mays, 42, 73 (top); Ted Spiegel, 45; Mitchell Gerber, 46 (top); Owen Franken, 46 (middle); Derick A. Thomas / Dat's Jazz, 46 (bottom); Hulton -Deutsch Collection, 47 (top); Bill Luster, 50; Donald C. Johnson, 59; Alain Le Garsmeur, 68; Charles E. Rotkin, 69 (top), 69 (bottom), 74; Randy Duchaine, 70; John Madere, 72 (top); H. David Seawell, 73 (bottom). *New York Public Library / Art Resource, NY:* 26. *Library of Congress (LC-USZ62-101923):* 22.

Book design by Anahid Hamparian

Printed in Italy

1   3   5   6   4   2

Contents

A Quick Look at Kentucky

Nickname: The Bluegrass State
Population: 4,041,769 (2000)
Statehood: 1792

Bird: Cardinal

The official state bird is the cardinal, which lives in the state throughout the year. Male cardinals have bright red feathers, while females are usually brown. Cardinals usually eat seeds, small wild fruits, and insects.

Flower: Goldenrod

The spiky yellow blossoms of the goldenrod can be found in many parts of the state. Historians believe that buffalo which roamed freely before the settlers arrived are partly responsible for spreading the flowers through the region. The goldenrod seeds would stick to the animals' fur and then fall off as the herds moved around.

Tree: Tulip Tree

The tulip tree is a member of the magnolia family. It has beautiful yellow-green flowers that bloom in the spring. Some tulip trees can live for more than one hundred years and grow to be more than 100 feet tall.

Horse: Thoroughbred

The thoroughbred is one of the fastest types of horses. Because of their speed they are often used for racing. Some adult thoroughbreds can weigh about 1,000 pounds and can be 5 feet high from the ground to their shoulders.

Animal: Gray Squirrel

The gray squirrel was declared the state animal in 1968. It can be found across most of the state, especially near nut-bearing trees. A member of the rodent family, this bushy-tailed squirrel is usually gray and white.

Fossil: Brachiopod

Brachiopods are the fossilized shells of creatures that lived in the oceans and seas. Kentucky and surrounding regions used to be underwater, so many different types of brachiopods can be found embedded in Kentucky rocks.

KENTUCKY

Mississippi River

Ohio River

Louisville

Frankfort

Licking River

Big Sandy River

Lexington

Paducah

Mammoth Cave National Park

Fort Knox

Kentucky River

Tug Fork River

Green River

Wickliffe Mounds

Kentucky Lake

Bowling Green

Lake Cumberland

Cumberland Gap National Historic Park

Black Mountain

Cumberland River

N

W   E

S

1 The Bluegrass State

Kentucky is located in the east central portion of the United States. Traveling by car, it would take approximately seven hours to drive across the state. But Kentucky is not a very large state. It has an area of about 40,000 square miles. Thirty-six other states are bigger than Kentucky, and only thirteen states are smaller.

Kentucky has an unusual shape. Its southern border is almost straight except for an interesting jut in the southwestern portion of the state. Three winding rivers— the Mississippi, Ohio, and Big Sandy Rivers—make the state's northern and western borders seem bumpy. The state's eastern border seems to have a sharp point jutting toward the east.

Kentucky's Borders
North: Illinois, Indiana, Ohio, the Ohio River, and the Big Sandy River
East: West Virginia and Virginia
South: Tennessee
West: Missouri and the Mississippi River

Kentucky has many different landscapes. To the east you will find a part of the Appalachian Mountains. The Appalachian Mountains stretch from Canada to Alabama, cutting through parts of southeastern Kentucky along the way. Big Black Mountain,

Sunlight filtering through the fog over the Appalachian hills

the state's highest point, can be found in this region. The mountain stands at 4,145 feet above sea level. The Cumberland Gap cuts through parts of the Appalachian Mountains, along the borders of Kentucky, Tennessee, and Virginia. Cumberland Gap National Historic Park is located there. The peaks and hills of the mountainous regions of Kentucky are covered in forests. You can also find deep valleys, gorges, rivers, and streams. Large coal deposits are another feature in this eastern section of Kentucky.

In the north-central portion of the state you will find flatter land. The land is not mountainous, but it does have rolling hills and valleys. The Kentucky River flows through this area, which is often called the Bluegrass Region. The soil there is fertile and many farms grow tobacco and corn. The region also has farms which raise livestock such as horses and

An aerial view of farms in Kentucky's north-central Bluegrass region

cattle. A large portion of the state's population lives in this region. Large cities such as Lexington and Louisville are located there. Frankfort, the state capital, is also in the Bluegrass Region.

To the south of the Bluegrass Region the land is relatively flat and is good for farming. But rocky ridges and raised bluffs can be found in this region as well. Stretching

Kentucky gets its nickname, the Bluegrass State, from the color of the grass that grows across the fertile areas of the state.

through southern, southeastern, and eastern parts of the state is the Daniel Boone National Forest. Covering nearly 700,000 acres of land, it is filled with cliffs, forests, lakes, and streams and is a popular attraction for people who want to enjoy the outdoors.

There are also many caves and lakes in southern Kentucky. Mammoth Cave National Park is located in the area. The cave system there is one of the most extensive on Earth. It was formed over millions of years as water ran down through the ground and wore away the limestone beneath. The system has interconnecting cave passageways that are

These strange formations found in Mammoth Cave are called stalactites. They are stone formations made from mineral deposits that have accumulated over thousands of years.

hundreds of miles long. Parts of Mammoth Cave are more than 300 feet below Earth's surface. Rivers and streams run through the cave system. Fish live in these dark waters and bats and other animals move through different parts of the caves. Artifacts such as tools and mummies have been found in Mammoth Cave, indicating that early Native Americans used the cave and its passageways. Later settlers also used and explored the caves. In the 1800s the caves were mined for products such as saltpeter, which was used in gunpowder. The United States government declared the region a national park in 1941. Today the cave system is preserved and visitors are welcome to explore parts of the caves. Mammoth Cave National Park is recognized as an official World Heritage Site because of its amazing natural features and its historical importance.

Western Kentucky has rolling fields ideal for farming. Plains and hills stretch westward, moving past the Mississippi River and beyond the state's borders. The region also has some swamps. Parts of western Kentucky have very large coal deposits. There is one small piece of Kentucky land—in the southwestern corner—that is cut off from the rest of the state by the Mississippi River. This very small region can be reached by road only from Tennessee.

Many rivers flow through Kentucky. The Mississippi and Ohio Rivers are two of the long rivers that flow around the borders of the state. Many smaller rivers cross Kentucky and run into the Ohio River. Fish swim through their waters and other wildlife live along their shores. Large boats travel on the state's rivers, carrying cargo between ports. Many of Kentucky's smaller rivers and streams run through rocky

The John A. Roebling Suspension Bridge stretches over the Ohio River, connecting Covington, Kentucky, with Cincinnati, Ohio.

gorges. Over the years, Kentuckians have built dams on many rivers in order to control the water flow and create electricity. These dams formed some of the state's lakes. In the western part of the state you will find man-made Kentucky Lake. It is more than 150 miles long. But the state also has natural lakes. Kentuckians come to these lakes to swim, boat, and fish. Birds and other animals live in and around the state's bodies of water.

In the United States there are only two very large waterfalls east of the Rocky Mountains. One is Niagara Falls in the north. The other is Cumberland Falls in Kentucky's Cumberland Falls State Resort Park. The waterfall is special not only for its size and beauty, but because a moonbow—a silver arc that crosses the sky over the falls—sometimes appears when the moon is full.

The falls at Cumberland Falls State Park

The leaves on the trees in the Daniel Boone National Forest change color as autumn progresses.

Climate

Because of its location, Kentucky has a temperate climate with rain in the spring, warm summers, dry fall weather, and cool winters. In the summertime, temperatures usually range from 70 to 80 degrees Fahrenheit. There have been times, however, when the summertime heat raises the temperature into the nineties and beyond. On average, winter temperatures are in the thirties.

Kentucky gets a lot of rain during the year, especially in the springtime. Snow also falls in the wintertime, with snowfall averages varying in different parts of the state. In the mountains in the northern part of the state there is enough snow for skiing during the cold months.

Kentucky Wildlife

Kentucky is home to many different plants and animals. Huge trees such as cypress grow along the rivers, while water plants grow in the shallow waters. The state has many forests. Hundreds of different types of trees grow there. They include elm, ash, hickory, maple, oak, cypress, cedar, hemlock, and pine. Today many of Kentucky's forests are second growth. This means that they are made up of new trees planted after the older and larger trees were cut down.

In the springtime wildflowers bloom across Kentucky's forests, mountainsides, and even along the highways. Plants such as jack-in-the-pulpit, goldenrod, Cumberland sandwort, and rosemary thrive in Kentucky's fertile soil. Mountain laurels, bluebells, rhododendrons, violets, azaleas, and bloodroot can also be found throughout the state.

The many different types of trees in My Old Kentucky Home State Park in Bardstown provide homes for many woodland plants and animals.

Plants & Animals

Bluegrass

This popular grass grows across the hills and fields of Kentucky. The grass is actually green in color, but at times the buds appear bluish. Bluegrass is not a plant that was native to Kentucky—it was imported years ago from Europe. For years, Kentuckians have been harvesting the grass seeds and selling them across the country and around the world.

White-Tailed Deer

These deer live in the forests, farmlands, and even around the suburban areas of Kentucky. A deer's coat can vary in color from brown to gray, but the underside of its tail is white. Fawns—or baby deer— have white spots to help them blend in with their surroundings.

Mink

A mink has a slender body and brown or black fur. It lives around lakes, rivers, marshes, and other bodies of water. It is an excellent swimmer and feeds on fish and small animals. For many years mink were hunted for their fur, but today mink farms breed the animals that are used for the fur products.

Bobcat

Bobcats can be found in the wooded areas of western Kentucky and the mountainous regions in the eastern part of the state. Bobcats in the Kentucky wilderness may grow to be about 3 feet long and can weigh around 30 pounds. They feed on small animals such as squirrels, rabbits, birds, and raccoons.

Saint John's Wort

This plant grows in the fields and forests in many parts of Kentucky. The plant can grow to be more than 1 foot tall, and has yellow flowers. Saint John's Wort is often used in herbal medicines.

Black Bear

Black bears live in forests and other wooded areas of Kentucky. These bears swim, climb trees, and can run quickly over short distances. They feed primarily on fruits, leaves, and other vegetation, but they also eat insects, fish, and small to medium-sized animals such as rodents or deer.

Before settlers came, Kentucky land had many different types of animals roaming freely. These included buffalo, wolves, cougars, and bears. Hunting and the loss of their natural habitat has decreased these animal populations, but the state still has many wild animals. Though there are no more wild buffalo roaming through the state, there are still wolves, bears, and cougars. Coyotes can also be found throughout the state, as can many deer. Small mammals also thrive in the Kentucky wilds. Raccoons, squirrels, and opossum live in the woods and fields.

The state's bodies of water are home to many different animals. River otters live along some of Kentucky's rivers and streams. Nature enthusiasts—as well as fishermen—can find catfish, bass, bluegill, perch, and trout in Kentucky's lakes, rivers, and streams. Kentucky's waters are also home to many types of reptiles and amphibians.

More than three hundred species—or types—of bird live in Kentucky. The biggest are birds of prey, which include bald eagles and hawks. Smaller birds such as bluejays, cardinals, chickadees, ducks, owls, pheasants, and geese can be found in the wilderness and around areas where many people live.

Protecting Nature

Throughout the years, Kentucky's wilderness—and the wildlife that lived in it—has disappeared. Settlers who made the state their home cut down many trees. When farming became popular, many forests were cleared to make fields and pastures. More forests and fields were used to build towns and cities. When the lumber industry became popular, thousands of trees were cut and sent down the rivers to be used and sold.

Raccoons can be found in the woods and the fields of Kentucky, though some live in urban and suburban areas.

Clear cutting the forests through the years has left mountain tops and hillsides bare and ugly.

Some of the animals that lived in these forests and fields managed to survive and live alongside humans and their settlements. Others disappeared forever. Today, however, Kentuckians are very aware of the need to preserve the natural wilderness found in their state. Kentucky has many state parks and wildlife and nature preserves. These places are protected by the government. The parks and preserves provide people with the chance to see the state's natural beauty, but they also give Kentucky's plants and animals space to grow and thrive. Additionally, Kentuckians are involved in different programs that increase the populations of specific plants and animals that are in danger of disappearing.

A great blue heron takes flight from a nature preserve.

2 From the Beginning

Before humans lived in the region now known as Kentucky, herds of animals such as mammoths (large animals that resembled furry elephants), musk oxen, and bison roamed through the land. About 12,000 years ago, humans came to the area. It is believed that they were hunters who followed the herds of mammoths or bison.

Two thousand years later, ancient people started to settle in Kentucky. They built villages along the area's rivers. Their houses were probably made of wood and dried mud. These early people lived off of the land and fished in the rivers, hunted large animals, and collected edible plants.

Around A.D. 800 to 1300, early native people who lived in the western area of the state built large mounds. These mounds were made of dirt and clay and were used as tombs and as places of religious worship. Inside these mounds archaeologists have found skeletal remains, as well as objects such as tools, pottery, and other valuables. Based on their research, archaeologists and scientists believe that these moundbuilders lived in well-organized

A young Kentuckian in the early 1900s

communities. They most likely grew and harvested corn and traded goods with other communities. Over time, however, the moundbuilders disappeared. Some scientists think that the moundbuilders might have joined other native cultures.

Wickliffe Mounds are located in western Kentucky near the Mississippi River. Researchers associated with Murray State University excavate and study the mound site and its artifacts. Visitors are welcome to visit the site and its museum during most of the year.

By the 1600s, Native American tribes living in the region included the Iroquois, Cherokee, Shawnee, and Chickasaw. The Cherokee lived in Kentucky's southeastern region. Some Cherokee lived in the mountainous areas of eastern Kentucky. Many lived in sturdy dwellings usually made of mud and clay, with roofs made of strong plants. The people grew food such as corn, squash, and beans, but also hunted deer and other animals. The Shawnee lived and hunted in parts of northern and central Kentucky. In western Kentucky, the Chickasaw established communities that grew crops and hunted local animals. Life for Kentucky's Native Americans began to change when European explorers and settlers arrived.

Many historians believe that Kentucky's name comes from a Native American word meaning "land of tomorrow" or "meadow land." But no one is sure from which tribe or nation the word originates.

Europeans Arrive

In the early 1670s, the Frenchmen Louis Jolliet and Jacques Marquette traveled down the Mississippi River. They believed that the river ended at the Pacific Ocean and could provide new and prosperous trade routes for France. They planned to claim the lands along the river for France. While traveling down the Mississippi, Jolliet and Marquette passed through parts of western Kentucky. There they met groups of Native Americans. Historians today believe that those natives were probably Shawnee.

In 1674, a British explorer named Gabriel Arthur entered Kentucky from the east. Despite this accomplishment, few traders or explorers at that time were eager to explore the new land. This was because the Appalachian Mountains were very hard to cross.

But exploration from the west continued. In 1682 the explorer Rene-Robert Cavalier, Sieur de La Salle (now commonly referred to as La Salle) traveled down the Mississippi by canoe. It is believed that during their travels La Salle and his men met Iroquois Indians from western Kentucky. La Salle and his men reached the end of the Mississippi, where the river empties into the Gulf of Mexico. La Salle claimed

La Salle claiming land along the Mississippi River for France

the lands along the Mississippi for France. Europeans considered the large region that included Kentucky as French property.

During the 1700s both France and Great Britain wanted to control the Ohio River and its surrounding lands. People living in Virginia—which was at that time a British colony—ignored French claims to areas around the Ohio River. Virginia's government encouraged its people to form land companies. These companies would help settlers move beyond the Appalachian Mountains into new land. Control over this land would make Virginia bigger and more powerful.

Thomas Walker, a doctor from Virginia, explored the Appalachian Mountains, looking for a safe and easy route to the West. In 1750, he found a passage through the low point in the Appalachian Mountains. Though Native Americans had used this route for centuries, this discovery was new to the colonists. This path came to be known as the Cumberland Gap. One year later, another man, Christopher Gist, explored northern Kentucky. Even though Walker and Gist told others that Kentucky was a very beautiful land, settlement there was still slow.

Despite the discovery of the Cumberland Gap, many people were afraid to leave their comfortable homes in Virginia for the wilderness beyond the Appalachian Mountains.

A picturesque view of the Cumberland Gap cutting through the Appalachian Mountains

The French and Indian War, which was fought between France and Great Britain, began in 1754. The fighting slowed exploration of Kentucky. At the end of the war, Great Britain won and gained the lands beyond the Appalachian Mountains. This included Kentucky. Explorers and hunters continued to venture into Kentucky. Daniel Boone, a famous hunter and explorer, traveled to Kentucky in 1769. This was the first of his many trips to the region.

In 1774, a group of colonists founded Harrodsburg. This settlement—the first permanent white settlement in Kentucky—was named after James Harrod, the leader of the group. In the beginning, the settlement was only a fort surrounded by a few cabins. The settlement eventually grew in size and population.

In 1775 Daniel Boone used the Cumberland Gap to lead settlers to Kentucky. The trail that he blazed—or established—was called the Wilderness Road. This route ended at the Ohio River, where the city of Louisville stands today. Boone established a fort along the Kentucky River. The site became known as Boonesborough. Many colonists followed Boone's Wilderness Road, settling down in different parts of Kentucky.

A reproduction of the log fort at Harrodsburg

Making a Model Log Cabin

Many settlers in Kentucky lived in log cabins made from the trees in the state's forests. By following these instructions you can make your own model log cabin.

What You Need

4 1/2 by 4 1/2-inch square piece of posterboard
Scissors with sharp points
9 by 10-inch piece of posterboard
Paintbrushes
Brown or tan tempera paint
Empty box from aluminum foil or plastic wrap
1 empty tissue box, 9 1/2 inches long and
    4 1/2 inches wide
Scotch tape
Extra posterboard scraps
Tacky glue (available in craft stores)
About 75 popsicle sticks (You can
    buy a box at a craft store)
Heavy phone book
Sandpaper

    Spread the newspapers on the table. Painting the cabin can be messy!

    Fold the small posterboard square in half diagonally and cut along the fold. Paint the two triangles brown or tan on one side and let them dry. These will be the ends of the roof.

    Fold the large piece of posterboard in half so it is 4 1/2 by 10 inches. Unfold and paint the outside brown. Use the paintbrush in short up-and-down strokes that look like shingles. This will be the peaked roof.

Use the foil box to make the chimney. Be very careful when handling the box. Most of these boxes have sharp edges. Stand the box on one end and cut it so it is about 2 inches taller than the tissue box when the tissue box is in its usual position. Ask an adult for help if it is too difficult to cut. Tape the foil box closed. Paint its sides brown. Let it dry. You may want to apply a second coat of paint later, to cover the printing.

Cut a doorway and window into one long side of the tissue box. With a scrap of posterboard, spread glue over one end of the tissue box. Cover that end with popsicle sticks, laid lengthwise, like cabin logs. Press them down firmly to make sure the sticks are glued well. Glue popsicle sticks lengthwise onto the other sides of the box. You will need to break some popsicle sticks to fit around the window and door. Here is an easy way to break a stick: Place one end under a phone book on the edge of a table or counter. Lean on the phone book and pull up sharply on the free end of the stick. Use sandpaper to smooth any rough edges.

While the glue is drying you can put the roof together. Open the roof so it forms an upside-down V, then stand it on one end so the V rests on the table. Fit a posterboard triangle inside, at the bottom, painted side down. Have someone hold the roof while you tape the two pieces together. Make sure to tape the pieces together on the inside so the tape will not show. Repeat on the other end of the roof. Set the roof on the cabin and tape the chimney to the side of the cabin.

When you are finished with your cabin, show it to your family and friends and try to imagine what life was like for a frontier family living in Kentucky.

In 1775 the Revolutionary War began. During the war, Native Americans who sided with the British attacked settlements in Kentucky. Settlers led by Boone and other Kentuckians defended their land. They were successful, but many Kentuckians died during the fighting.

The Revolutionary War ended in 1783. This meant that the colonies were no longer controlled by Great Britain. Kentucky was still considered a part of Virginia. At that time, the population of Kentucky was only 12,000. But over the next twenty years, around 100,000 new settlers arrived. By 1792, Kentucky had enough people to become a state of its own. Kentucky became the fifteenth state on June 1, 1792. Frankfort became the capital city.

Settlers head toward the lands of Kentucky.

Boats traveling down the Ohio River past the busy Louisville port.

During the early years of statehood, most Kentuckians made their living from the land. They grew and harvested crops on farms across the state. Some of the products grown included corn, tobacco, rye, and hemp—which was used to make rope. Over time, Kentucky's towns and cities began to grow in size and population. Louisville, which was located along the Ohio River became an important trade center and port. At first, rafts and flatboats—square boats with flat bottoms—were used to move goods along the Ohio River. Steamboats were later used to move cargo and passengers down the rivers. Farmers brought their crops to Louisville. From there, the crops were sent down the Ohio and Mississippi Rivers to places such as New Orleans. From New Orleans, the crops could be sent to states on the Atlantic Coast or to countries in Central America, South America, or Europe.

The Civil War

In 1861, the Civil War began. But problems had been brewing for years over issues such as slavery. The southern economy was dependent upon agriculture. Large plantations required many workers and plantation owners used slaves to work in the fields. For the people of the South, slavery was an important part of their lives. By contrast, the North did not have the same need for slaves. Some Northerners also felt that slavery was morally wrong.

Eleven southern states left the United States and formed a new nation called the Confederate States of America. The states that did not leave the United States were a part of the Union. Kentucky did not join the Confederacy. Though the state was officially a part of the Union, many Kentuckians sympathized

Union troops cross over a bridge near Columbus, Kentucky, in 1861.

Kentucky

Confederate and Union forces fight during the Battle of Munfordville.

with the South. Many plantation owners in Kentucky also depended upon slave labor to maintain the crops. Supporters of the South formed a Confederate government in Bowling Green, despite the fact that the state was officially part of the Union. The government only lasted for a short period of time.

But men from Kentucky fought on both sides in the Civil War. Around 30,000 Kentuckians fought for the Confederacy. Nearly 75,000 Kentucky citizens fought for the North. Battles were fought on Kentucky soil. Some of the battles ended in Union victory, while the

During the Civil War, Jefferson Davis served as the president for the Confederacy and Abraham Lincoln was the president of the Union. Both men were born in Kentucky.

Confederates triumphed in others. But the fighting took a toll on the land and the people of Kentucky.

After the War

In 1865, the Civil War ended. The Confederate states returned to the Union. For a time, the economy of Kentucky suffered. Before the war, the farmers of the state had sold many of their crops to other Southerners. After the war, most southern states did not have much money to spend on Kentucky produce.

From the 1870s to early 1900s, the state's economy started to improve. Tobacco continued to be an important crop in

During the 1870s Kentucky's economy improved and boats and trains brought goods to and from the state's growing cities.

Kentucky. Coal mines in Kentucky also helped the economy. Trains were fueled by coal, and more railroads were being built across America. Demand for Kentucky coal increased.

Hard Times

World War I, which lasted from 1914 to 1918, affected the economy and people of the United States. Many states, including Kentucky, provided products for the troops fighting in the war, but the economy still suffered. Several Kentuckians were also killed in this war.

The 1920s were a difficult time for many farms across the country. Farm products sold for less and many farmers had a hard time maintaining their farms. When the Great Depression hit the United States in 1929, Kentuckians suffered as did most other Americans. Jobs were very hard to find and many people could not make enough to pay for their homes and feed their families. Many coal miners lost their jobs and farms across the state failed.

A mining family in 1929

A family living along the Kentucky River in 1940

Kentucky's economy improved during World War II, which lasted from 1939 to 1945. Food and supplies were in demand and farms and mines in Kentucky again became prosperous. Factories which produced war supplies were built across the state. The growth in industry provided many Kentuckians with much-needed jobs.

In Fort Knox in 1936, the U.S. Treasury Department created a depository—a type of storage center—for gold and other government valuables. Today Fort Knox holds billions of dollars worth of gold and important documents such as the Declaration of Independence and the Constitution.

During the mid 1900s, segregation became a major issue for Kentuckians. For years, African-American Kentuckians were legally prohibited from using many of the same facilities as white people. African-American school children were schooled separately from white children and many African-American men and women were denied jobs for which they were qualified. African-American and some white Kentuckians protested these laws. Demonstrations were held in different Kentucky cities and towns. The laws slowly changed. In 1948 Louisville allowed African Americans to use the public library. Soon after that, African Americans were allowed to join the police force and fire departments. In 1956 the city announced it was going to desegregate its public schools. But in reality, very few schools were fully desegregated. In 1963 the city council of Louisville passed a law that stated that race discrimination was not allowed in the city. Louisville was one of the first Southern cities to pass such a law. Similar legislation was attempted across the state with mixed

A desegregated high school in Louisville in the 1950s

results. Some people in Kentucky still believed in segregation and the fight for equality continued into the 1970s.

During the mid-1960s, Kentucky and other parts of Appalachia gained national attention when President Lyndon B. Johnson began the program he called his War on Poverty. Though many Kentuckians lived in areas of tremendous mineral wealth, they were often very poor. Federal programs were created to try to help people escape poverty. Such efforts continue to this day.

. . . [T]he wealth produced by coal and timber was seldom seen locally. It went downstream with the great hardwood logs; it rode out on rails with the coal cars; it was mailed between distant cities . . . Even the wages [earnings] of local miners returned to faraway stockholders [through] company houses and company stores.

—A portion of a report on poverty written for President Lyndon B. Johnson

In the late twentieth century, the state changed in many ways. The coal industry went into a decline. In 1990, there were fifty thousand fewer miners in Appalachia than there were ten years earlier. But the state population continues to grow and different industries continue to come to the state to provide some jobs and services for the people.

Kentucky—much like other states in the country—still faces problems such as unemployment, poverty, and environmental concerns. But Kentuckians are working hard to fix these problems. They hope to create a bright and prosperous future for their state.

Important Dates

A.D. 800-1300   Moundbuilding culture flourishes in parts of Kentucky.

1600s   Cherokee, Chickasaw, and Shawnee tribes live and hunt in the region.

1674   British Explorer Gabriel Arthur enters Kentucky from the east.

1682   French Explorer Rene-Robert Cavalier, Sieur de La Salle travels down the Mississippi River and passes through Kentucky. He eventually claims land along the Mississippi River for France.

La Salle

1750   Thomas Walker discovers a pathway through the Appalachian Mountains that would later be called the Cumberland Gap.

1751   Christopher Gist explores parts of northern Kentucky along the Ohio River.

1774   Harrodsburg becomes the first permanent white settlement in Kentucky.

1775   Daniel Boone blazes the Wilderness Road, creating an easier route for settlers moving to Kentucky.

1775   Fort Boonesborough is founded along the southern part of the Kentucky River.

1792   Kentucky becomes the fifteenth state.

1809   Abraham Lincoln is born near Hodgenville.

1810   Steamboats begin to carry goods down the Mississippi River.

1861-1865 The Civil War is fought. During the war Kentucky remains a part of the Union, but residents fight on both sides.

Daniel Boone

1930s   The Great Depression hurts Kentucky's economy and many residents are left unemployed.

1936   Fort Knox becomes a major depository for gold and other government valuables.

1966   Kentucky becomes the first southern state to pass a civil rights act, granting African Americans equal rights.

1983   Martha Layne Collins is elected Kentucky's first woman governor.

1980s   Automobile manufacturing plants are built in the state, providing jobs for many residents.

1990   The state supreme court orders the government to create a new public school system that is fair to both rural and urban districts.

1992   Kentucky celebrates the bicentennial of its statehood.

3 The People

The state of Kentucky is growing and changing. In 1990, the census showed that the state had a population of 3,685,296. By 2000, the population had increased to 4,041,769. Although four million may seem like a lot of people, Kentucky's population is not very large when compared to other states. Almost half of the other states have larger populations than Kentucky.

In the past, the largest number of people who lived in Kentucky were Caucasian. This remains true today. The 2000 census showed that 90 percent of the state's population was white. African Americans made up about 7 percent, while Hispanic and Latino residents made up 1.5 percent of the population. Asians and Asian Americans represented less than 1 percent of the population. There were even fewer Native Americans living in Kentucky.

The Caucasians living in the state have different backgrounds. Some are the descendants of European and American pioneers who settled in Kentucky. Over the years Americans from

Children on a playground in Georgetown

other parts of the country have made Kentucky their home. Kentucky also has families who come from countries such as Ireland, Germany, Scotland, or England.

One group of Caucasian settlers who lived in Kentucky was a religious group called the Shakers. The Shakers originally came from Great Britain and believed in a type of Christianity that practiced separation from the rest of the world. During the mid-1800s Kentucky Shakers established settlements near Harrodsburg and Bowling Green. They lived in close-knit communities, but often interacted and traded with non-Shaker

Shaker Village of Pleasant Hill, near Harrodsburg, is a restored Shaker community complete with reproductions of nineteenth-century buildings and acres of farmland. Visitors are welcome to explore the village and learn about Shaker culture and history.

Men dressed in traditional Shaker clothing drive an oxcart in Shaker Village at Pleasant Hill.

communities nearby. Many Shakers were farmers or craftspeople. Shaker furniture and crafts are well known and prized around the world. But today there are very few Shakers living in the United States.

Ethnic Diversity

Many Africans and African Americans first came to Kentucky as slaves. After the Civil War ended, these slaves were freed. But anti-black sentiment was still active in parts of Kentucky and many blacks had trouble finding jobs and maintaining their own land. Some African-American families were able to own their homes and manage their own farms, but many more were forced to live in poverty. Young African-American children

This African-American couple from the 1890s owned the land upon which they built their cabin.

often could not attend school and enjoy benefits that other Kentucky children had.

This discrimination continued into the 1900s. But African Americans still remained an important part of Kentucky's history. Kentucky's African Americans helped to build and fill the state's bustling cities. Many also worked in the coal mines and at other jobs that helped boost the state's economy in the 1940s. Conditions started to improve in the 1950s and 1960s, when people throughout the state started pushing for equal rights for Kentucky's black population. Change was slow to come and racial tensions still exist. But today many African Americans in Kentucky are able to live successful and prosperous lives. They are an important part of the state's workforce. Many run their own businesses and take part in state and local government.

Kentucky's Hispanic population continues to grow. Many immigrants are coming from Mexico and other countries in Central and South America. Some of these newcomers have come to Kentucky looking for better opportunities for themselves and for their families. Kentucky's Hispanics often work on farms, in factories, and in other businesses. Many also own their own businesses. Some families have established restaurants and stores that offer food and products from their homeland. Many of Kentucky's Hispanic residents take an active part in community and government activities.

> *Here [in Kentucky] I have work, I have money, I have free time, I have a lot of different opportunities . . . In Mexico, I worked just to eat.*
> —Miguel Caballero, a Mexican immigrant explaining why he lives in Kentucky

The people who come to Kentucky from other countries bring along their culture and traditions. Their experiences and contributions have helped to make Kentucky what it is today.

Native Americans

Before white settlers and explorers came to Kentucky, the region's population was all Native American. But today they make up a very small part of the population. As white settlers came to Kentucky, Native Americans had less land on which they could farm and hunt. In some instances the Native Americans were forcibly removed from lands their ancestors had inhabited for centuries. Some Native Americans in Kentucky also married American and European settlers or joined their communities.

An Indian-American woman performs a Hindu dance for Kentuckians. People from many different cultures share their heritage at events held across the state.

There are no Native American reservations in Kentucky today. But this does not mean that the Native Americans are not an active part of the state's society. Festivals and other traditional gatherings are held across the state. Native Americans use these events to celebrate and honor their heritage, but the events also offer Kentucky residents and visitors a chance to learn more about Native American history and culture.

Famous Kentuckians

Diane Sawyer: Journalist

Born in Glasgow, Kentucky, in 1945, Diane Sawyer began her broadcasting career at a television station in Louisville. Now an award-winning journalist, Sawyer has investigated and reported on issues such as biological weapons, racial discrimination, child abuse, famine, and corruption. She has interviewed American and international political figures and has reported from many other countries. She currently anchors—or hosts—investigative news and morning television shows.

Colonel Harland Sanders: Businessman

The Colonel's career in cooking started when he cooked food for people who passed by his service station in Corbin. He opened a restaurant that served his food and eventually sold his famous fried chicken to other restaurants. In 1935 Kentucky's governor made Sanders a Kentucky Colonel for his "contribution to the state's cuisine." He sold his business to a major corporation in 1964 and Kentucky Fried Chicken became world famous. Sanders died in 1980.

Lionel Hampton: Musician

Lionel Hampton was born in Louisville. He played the drums, worked as a band leader, and performed with other music legends such as Benny Goodman. Hampton is credited with increasing the popularity of the vibraphone in jazz performances. Hampton died in 2002.

Muhammad Ali: Boxer

Cassius Clay was born in Louisville in 1942. In 1964 he changed his name to Muhammad Ali when he began practicing Islam. Ali is an American heavy-weight boxing champion who has won many titles, but is also famous for his colorful character and some of the controversy that surrounded his career. Today Ali has Parkinson's disease and can no longer box, but he dedicates much of his time to charitable causes.

Henry Clay: Politician and Orator

Though he was born in Virginia, Henry Clay spent many years practicing law in Kentucky. He was elected to the state legislature in 1803 and later served in the U.S. House of Representatives and the U.S. Senate. During his political career he made many stirring speeches and settled many disputes between the North and South and between the United States and other countries. Clay was given the nickname the Great Compromiser for his efforts.

Emma C. Clement: American Mother-of-the-Year

In 1946, Emma C. Clement was honored as the American Mother-of-the-Year. She was the first African American to receive the award. Clement was the granddaughter of a slave and believed in equal rights for all African Americans. When she received the award, the college graduate and mother of seven said that she was accepting it on behalf of all mothers and on behalf of millions of African Americans in the United States.

Until the 1960s, most Kentuckians lived in rural areas. Today, however, more than half live in a town or city. But only Lexington and Louisville have populations of more than 200,000. Some of the other cities in the state are Owensboro, Covington, Bowling Green, Hopkinsville, Frankfort, Paducah, Henderson, and Richmond.

Downtown Louisville has many historic buildings, some of which are more than 150 years old. But modern buildings such as skyscrapers can be found in the city. Every spring thousands of visitors come to the city to watch the Kentucky Derby.

The other towns and cities in Kentucky have their own history, traditions, and festivals. Some towns are on the out-skirts of the cities and have malls, large office buildings, and

A soccer game played on a field in Lexington

Young Kentuckians learn about how settlers who lived in Kentucky towns raised sheep.

other urban features. Other towns are further into the countryside. Several towns were established for miners, loggers, and their families. But some of these towns suffered when mines closed and workers lost their jobs. People left their houses or stores and towns appeared abandoned.

Life in the Appalachian Mountains of Kentucky can be very hard. Yet many Kentuckians enjoy living in the mountains. In many cases, their families have lived in the region for generations. One reason mountain life is hard is because these people live in remote locations. Many families live far from towns and other families. They may have to travel a great distance to reach stores and schools. Because of the terrain, there are not many jobs in the mountainous part of the state. Many people living in the region work in the mines, which can be very dangerous work. But despite their worries, the people of Appalachia appreciate living in a place of great beauty and serenity.

Fun in Kentucky

Kentuckians have many fun ways to enjoy themselves. Kentucky does not have professional basketball or football teams, but Kentuckians are proud of their minor league baseball team. Many residents are also fans of college and university sports teams. They often attend many games to cheer on the athletes.

Kentuckians of all ages enjoy cheering for their home teams.

Many come to Kentucky to enjoy the outdoors. The state has parks and recreation areas. Hiking, camping, boating, and fishing are popular pastimes for residents and visitors alike. Others come from all over to enjoy the festivals and fairs that are held throughout the year in different parts of the state.

These boys play on a rope bridge at the Daniel Boone National Forest.

Visitors to Louisville can visit the Louisville Slugger Museum.

Kentucky

Kentucky has many museums and other centers where visitors can learn about such things as the state's history and culture. People interested in Kentucky history can also tour the many historic sites, such as the homes of famous Kentuckians or locations of historic battles.

The Kentucky Derby is arguably the most popular event in the state. This horse race has been held in Louisville every May since 1875. Thousands of people come to watch. Weeks before the race, Louisville hosts the Kentucky Derby Festival, which includes fireworks, concerts, parades, and exhibitions.

All in all, Kentucky has a lot to offer everybody.

Fast horses at the Kentucky Derby

Calendar of Events

Gathering of Eagles

Every January Kentucky Dam Village State Resort Park in southwestern Kentucky, hosts this event. Visitors are given the opportunity to view bald eagles in their natural habitat.

Native American Weekend

In January visitors can travel to Lake Cumberland State Resort Park to learn about Native American life and culture.

The Kentucky Derby Festival

For two weeks in April, right before the Kentucky Derby, Louisville becomes a center of community activity. The festival has fireworks, races, concerts, and other fun activities. Proceeds of the festival benefit the local economy and local charities.

Apple Blossom Festival

This event is held in Elkhorn City every May. A parade, craft booths, music, local art, and food are a part of this celebration of springtime in the mountains.

Boone Day

Every year on June 7, the Kentucky Historical Society in Frankfort celebrates the day when Daniel Boone first viewed Kentucky from the Cumberland Gap. Visitors learn about the history, folklore, culture, and people of early Kentucky.

Highland Games in Glasgow

Scottish culture and traditions are honored at this June festival. Members of different Scottish clans from across the country meet to enjoy the Scottish music and athletic events.

An air show during the Kentucky Derby Festival

Fireworks during a festival

Official Kentucky State Championship Old-time Fiddlers Contest

Every July musicians from across the country come to the city of Falls of Rough to compete in this event. Besides fiddling contests, the event also features harmonica, banjo, and jig dancing competitions.

Kentucky State Fair

This annual August event is held at the Louisville State Fairgrounds. Each year more than 600,000 people go to the fair to enjoy the contests, music performances, rides, games, food, and more.

Festival of the Horse

The city of Georgetown hosts this annual September celebration. Parades, a carnival, entertainment, and other activities celebrate the horse's importance in Kentucky history and culture.

Trail of Tears Powwow

The long journey that Cherokees were forced to endure when they were moved from their native lands to Oklahoma from 1838 to 1839, was called the Trail of Tears. Hopkinsville, Kentucky, was one of the places where they stopped along the way. A commemorative park in the city is the site of this annual September celebration of Native American history and culture.

4 How It Works

In Kentucky, as in other states, government exists at different levels. The local government of cities and towns is called municipal government. Local governments are usually run by officials who go by such titles as mayor, city manager, or council member. It is the responsibility of the local leaders to make sure that their city or town runs well. One important duty is listening to residents or community groups who have issues with the local government or local laws. A mayor or city manager would also have to focus on the public school system for his or her town or city.

Though Kentucky is one of the fifty states, it is also known as a commonwealth. Pennsylvania, Massachusetts, and Virginia are also called commonwealths.

Towns and cities are grouped according to location. These groups are called counties. Kentucky has 120 counties. Kentucky counties are run by a governing body called the fiscal court, which includes a county judge and commissioners. County government is especially important in sparsely populated places, where many people live outside of towns and

This statue of William Goebel, the thirty-fourth governor of the state, stands in Frankfort.

Branches of Government

Executive The governor is the highest-ranking official in the state. The governor serves a four-year term. He or she is responsible for signing bills into law after the legislature has approved them. The governor must also work on a state budget.

Legislative The legislative branch makes state laws. The state legislature is called the General Assembly, and is broken down into two divisions: the senate and the house of representatives. There are thirty-eight state senators and one hundred state representatives.

Judicial The judicial branch is made up of four different court systems: district courts, circuit courts, court of appeals, and the supreme court. District courts are mainly for county matters or civil matters that involve less than $4,000. Circuit courts are for civil matters concerning more than $4,000 and also hear appeals from district courts. The court of appeals hears appeals from the circuit courts. The supreme court is the highest court and hears certain appeals.

cities. These people depend more on county governments to help them, since they do not have a town government to do so.

The state government is the next level of Kentucky government. The state government is broken down into three branches. These branches work together to make and carry out state laws.

Offices of the state government are located in Frankfort. Kentuckians often boast that their capitol building is among

Flowers bloom in front of the Kentucky capitol.

the most beautiful in the United States. The governor's mansion is also located in the capital.

Martha Layne Collins became the state's first woman governor in 1983.

How a Bill Becomes a Law

A state law first starts out as a bill. The idea for the bill can come from state legislators or from the people they represent. However, only representatives or senators can formally introduce a bill into the house or senate. After the bill is introduced to either the house or senate it is given a number and assigned

A fully-functioning clock, covered in flowers, is located in Frankfort. All the flowers used for the clock are grown in Kentucky.

A view of the interior of the dome at Frankfort's Old State Capitol

to a committee. This committee discusses the bill. If committee members are in favor of the bill, the bill has a first reading and will move on for a second reading. After the second reading, the bill is sent to the Rules Committee. When it is approved by the Rules Committee it is then presented to the entire senate or house of representatives (depending upon where the bill originated.) All the members of the house or senate discuss, debate, or amend—change—the bill. If it is approved by two-fifths of the members, the bill is sent on to the other house.

Once in the other house, the bill moves through the same process. If both houses pass the bill, it is read again and prepared for the governor. Both houses must agree on the final version of the bill. Once in the governor's hands, the bill can be rejected or approved. Even if the governor rejects—or vetoes—it, the bill can still be passed if a majority of the members of both houses are still in approval.

Getting Involved

Kentuckians get involved in politics and government at different levels. Some run for election to political office. Others choose to participate in other ways. The way that most people participate is by making their voices heard. Elected government officials are supposed to represent the people who elect them. Sometimes officials hold meetings and invite voters to attend and to speak their minds. Another way to get involved is to write to your state representatives or senators.

Here is an example of how Kentucky residents made a difference. In 1998, a coal company wanted to start strip mining on Black Mountain. Strip mining involves clearing off

To find contact information for Kentucky's state legislators go to this Web site:
http://www.lrc.state.ky.us/whoswho/whoswho.htm
In order to find your representatives or senators, you need to know what district you belong to. Your parents, teachers, or librarians can help you find your district.

everything above a coal deposit. This would include all of the plants and wildlife that lived there. The company's plans were announced in newspapers and on television. Children who lived close to the mountain and attended Wallins Creek School in Harlan County were upset by the news. They wanted to do something to stop the mining. They started a protest. The students also raised money so that they could spend two days to study the plants and animals that lived on the mountain. While on this field trip, they talked to other people who lived nearby. The students also visited other strip mining sites. Once they had gathered all of their information, they started to write and to speak about what they had learned. At community meetings, they told adult voters about the reasons they thought the strip mining should not be allowed. They also sent e-mails and letters to government officials.

By the year 2000, coal companies reached an agreement with the state government. The coal companies would leave the top of Black Mountain alone. Plans for a conservation area are underway. This success shows that the opinions of young Kentuckians matter.

5 Making a Living

Today the people in Kentucky make their money in many different ways. In 2000, Kentucky had almost two million workers. About one out of every four Kentuckians worked in service industries such as real estate, finance, retail, or insurance. More than one hundred thousand people held government jobs. The same number worked in factories. Fewer people worked in farming, forestry, fishing, construction, and mining.

Wealth from the Land

The plants that grow in Kentucky's fertile soil have brought profit to the state's residents. One crop that has had a long history in the state is tobacco. Historians say that Native Americans living in the area thousands of years ago smoked the tobacco that grew wild there. Early white settlers also grew tobacco, which they sent to factories in Louisville, where it was made into cigars, snuff, and chewing and pipe tobacco. Once cigarettes became popular, tobacco became Kentucky's most important crop. In recent years, however, Americans have

A young girl helps out on a horse farm in Lexington.

become more aware of the dangers related to tobacco use. As a result, the demand for tobacco is not as high as it once was. Though there are still tobacco farms and factories across the state, the future for those industries—and the workers—may not be bright. Some farmers who once grew tobacco are trying to find other crops to grow.

Farms across the state grow crops such as corn, wheat, hay, and soybeans. Other farmers in parts of Kentucky specialize in poultry that will be sold as food. Breeding and selling beef cattle is also an important source of income for Kentucky.

A tobacco field near Hopkinsville

Kentucky

Making Baked Grits

Grits are a traditional southern treat. They are ground hominy, which are kernels of corn that have been soaked until the hulls are removed. This recipe adds zip to the popular dish.

1 cup quick-cooking grits
2 cups sharp cheddar cheese, grated
1-1/2 teaspoons minced garlic
4 tablespoons melted butter
1/2 cup chopped green onion
2 eggs
3/4 cups milk

Ask an adult to help you prepare the grits. You should follow the cooking instructions on the package of grits.

When the grits are done, stir in the cheese, garlic, butter, and chopped onions. Pour the grits mixture into a greased casserole dish. Set this aside for now.

In a small dish lightly beat the eggs. Stir in the milk. Pour the milk and egg mixture over the grits. Bake for 1 hour at 375 degrees. Be sure to have an adult help you with the oven. When the baking is complete, carefully remove the dish from the oven and allow it to cool for a little while. When the grits are cool enough to eat, dig in and enjoy!

Horses graze peacefully on a horse farm.

Another animal that is bred in Kentucky is the Thoroughbred horse; but unlike other livestock, these animals are not used for food. The bluegrass region of Kentucky has many horse farms. On many horse farms white fences surround huge pastures where horses graze on the lush grass. These horses are bred and sold within the state and around the country. Many of the horses are used for racing and riding competitions. The thoroughbred trade makes a lot of money for the state.

Another industry that uses Kentucky land is mining. For a long time coal was an important mineral for Kentucky. It was needed to fuel trains and steamboats and to heat buildings and factories. Mining is still important to Kentucky's economy. Kentucky is one the country's leading coal producers.

The two main sources of coal can be found in the eastern and western sections of the state. But mining is very difficult and dangerous work. Miners often work very long hours in dangerous conditions. The dust and fumes in the mines are also hazardous to their health.

Heavy-duty trucks haul Kentucky products such as coal and other minerals.

Despite how profitable the industry is, coal mining is bad for Kentucky land. Strip mining does nearly irreparable damage to the land. Coal mining also causes erosion and pollutes the state's water. Once the coal in a particular mine is gone, the mine is no longer useful and the land remains scarred and open. In some instances, however, coal companies have tried to restore the land they mined. Trees and other plants are replaced and efforts are made to remove pollution from the area. This sometimes works, but in many cases, bare patches of mined land remain ruined and empty.

When all the coal was removed from the land shown here, the soil was replaced and the plants and the trees were replanted.

Making Things

For a long time farming and mining were the main industries of Kentucky. But by the 1930s, manufacturing became profitable. After 1945, there was a huge increase in factory jobs. New industries came to Kentucky because of its large supply of coal and the low cost of electricity. Within fifty years,

This Kentucky factory is famous for making Louisville Slugger bats.

manufacturing became Kentucky's major source of income.

A large number of people in Kentucky work in factories. The biggest factories in the state make automobiles and appliances. Kentucky factories also produce chemicals, electrical equipment, food products, textiles, metal products, and bourbon whiskey. Besides bringing income into the state with the sale of the manufactured products, these factories also provide jobs for many Kentuckians.

Though factories make most Kentucky products, some items are still handmade. During the state's early history, Kentuckians had to make many of the things they used every day. Families made their own furniture, including beds, tables, and rocking chairs. Women wove rugs and sewed the quilts their families used. Some Kentuckians whittled toys and fishing rods, while others made clay pots. Kentuckians also made folk art, such as paintings and sculptures. Not only are Kentucky's arts and crafts symbols of the state's history, but they are also profitable. Many Kentucky craftspeople make a living by selling the beautiful objects they create.

Tourism

Tourism is a growing industry in Kentucky. People come from all over the world to visit Kentucky. Many of them come to see horse races such as the Kentucky Derby. Others come to the state's fantastic natural wonders, including Cumberland Falls, Mammoth Cave, and the state's parks and forests.

The money that people spend when visiting Kentucky is good for the economy. The jobs created by tourism help Kentuckians make a living. Some residents work in the hotels, restaurants, and shops that tourists visit. Others are tour guides or work in one of the state's many museums.

Annual events that attract many tourists—such as the Kentucky Derby—are good for the state's economy.

Products & Resources

Kentucky's chemicals are one of the state's most profitable manufactured products. Paints and cleaning chemicals are just two of the types of chemicals produced in Kentucky. Pharmaceutical chemicals are also made in the state's chemical plants.

Cattle

Livestock farms across the state raise the beef cattle that will be sent around the country. According to the Kentucky Cattlemen's Association, of all the states east of the Mississippi River, Kentucky produces the most cattle.

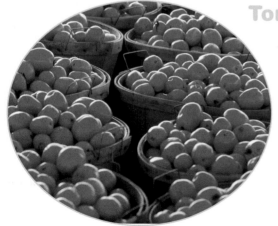

Tomatoes

Fruits and vegetables grow in farms in every part of the state. Kentucky's tomato crop is important to the state's agricultural economy.

Electric Power

Though most of Kentucky's energy comes from coal, hydroelectric power is also important. Hydroelectric power is created by using dams and other devices to control the flows of many of Kentucky's waterways.

Corn

Corn fields can be found in different parts of the state. However, much of the corn grown in Kentucky is turned into feed for the livestock raised on farms.

Steel

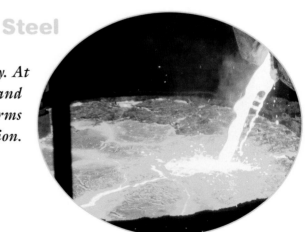

Steel is manufactured in Kentucky. At steel plants, workers melt the metal and make it into bars, sheets, and other forms that can be used for construction.

Finding a Balance

Humans have lived off Kentucky land for thousands of years. Sometimes humans were able to use the land without doing too much damage. But in many cases the land and environment have suffered from human industries. Chemical plants and other factories often release toxic waste into the state's land and water. As a result, the wildlife suffers. Pollution has also harmed crops and livestock. In some cases humans have become sick from the pollution. But this is not a simple issue. Kentucky's industries have brought great wealth and prosperity to the state. Without factories and plants many Kentuckians would be unemployed and unable to support themselves and their families.

Many corporations have agreed to be more careful about the pollution that comes from their factories. The state also has recycling programs that encourage residents to be more careful and respectful of the environment. As the state moves toward the future, the people will continue to strike a balance between humans and nature so that Kentucky can remain beautiful and safe.

Toxic waste and other pollutants from factories and chemical plants have been released onto Kentucky's land and into its water.

Kentuckians work hard to find ways to balance the state's needs so that Kentucky can continue to be the best that it can be.

The state flag consists of the state seal on a navy blue background.

The state seal shows a frontiersman and a statesman shaking hands. The state motto, "United We Stand Divided We Fall" is printed around the two men. The outer border of the seal displays the words Commonwealth of Kentucky and a wreath of goldenrod.

Kentucky

My Old Kentucky Home

Words and Music by Stephen Collins Foster

The sun shines bright in the old Ken-tuck-y Home; 'Tis sum-mer, the peo-ple, are gay. The corn-top's ripe and the mead-ow's in the bloom, While the birds make mu-sic all the day. The young folks roll on the lit-tle cab-in floor; All mer-ry, all hap-py, and bright. By'n by Hard Times comes a knock-ing at the door; Then, my old Ken-tuck-y Home, Good-night!

Chorus

Weep no more, my la-dy. Oh, weep no more to-day. We will sing one song for the old Ken-tuck-y Home; For the old Ken-tuck-y Home, far-a-way.

More About Kentucky

Books

Boraas, Tracey. *Daniel Boone: Frontier Scout.* Mankato, MN: Capstone
Press, 2002.

Brown, Dottie. *Kentucky.* Minneapolis, MN: Lerner Publishing, 2002.

Smith, Adam and Katherine S. Smith. *A Historical Album of Kentucky.*
Brookfield, CT: Millbrook Press, 1995.

Thompson, Kathleen. *Kentucky.* Austin, TX: Raintree Steck-Vaughn, 1996.

Web sites

Official Kentucky State Web site:

www.kentucky.gov

Kentucky Tourism:

www.kytourism.com

About the Author

Ann Graham Gaines is a freelance writer and picture researcher, whose first
book for children was published in 1991. She and her family live near Gonzales,
Texas. Kentucky is one of her favorite places to visit.

Index

Page numbers in **boldface** are illustrations.